Well-controlled clinical research proves phosphatidylserine (PS) has more universal, holistic benefits for the brain than any other nutrient or drug. Taken as a dietary supplement, PS is a key building block for nerve cells. By building cell membranes, PS revitalizes the cells of the brain. Connections are formed; circuits are rebuilt. Seventeen double-blind trials prove that PS helps improve the brain's electrical rhythms and reverses age-related memory decline, notably in people with Alzheimer's and dementia; eases anxiety and lifts depression; benefits motor functions in Parkinson's patients; and generally improves learning, concentration and word skills. Able to enhance brain function in young and old, and with proven safety and tolerability, this powerful nutrient can help turn back the clock on aging.

Parris M. Kidd, Ph.D. was trained in the life sciences at the University of the West Indies and at the University of California at Berkeley and its San Francisco Medical Center. He has applied his exceptionally broad research and teaching experience to nutrition since 1983, when he authored a landmark textbook on free radicals and antioxidant nutrients. Since 1987 he has been researching phospholipid nutrients and their benefits as cell membrane orthomolecules. Dr. Kidd has published and lectured on a wide variety of topics, and is internationally recognized as a foremost scientific authority on nutrition and human health.

Phosphatidylserine (PS): Number-One Brain Booster

The nutrient building block that accelerates all brain functions and counters Alzheimer's

Parris M. Kidd, Ph.D.

Keats Publishing, Inc. New Canaan, Connecticut

Phosphatidylserine is not intended as medical advice. Its intent is solely informational and educational. Please consult a health professional if you have questions about your health.

PHOSPHATIDYLSERINE

Keats Good Herb Guides are published by
Keats Publishing, Inc.
27 Pine Street (Box 876)
New Canaan, Connecticut 06840-0876

Keats Publishing website address: www.keats.com

Contents

The decline of mental capacity with age is the new challenge to health care. Humans now live longer than ever before, but of every four Americans who make it past 85 years of age, it is likely that two will be suffering from Alzheimer's or other severe mental deterioration when they die. The public perception of Alzheimer's is not inflated: many of these poor souls die without dignity, unaware of who they are and unable to recognize loved ones as their lives fade away. This is a very important problem for all of us to face up to, for without our minds, what are we?

Science has risen to this challenge. Its answer for slowing, in some cases even for reversing, mental decline is lifestyle revision and dietary supplementation with the nutrient phosphatidylserine (called PS for short).

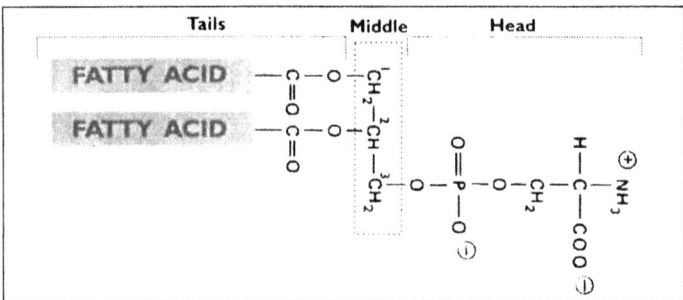

Figure 1. The molecular structure of phosphatidylserine (PS).

PS is a key building block for all the billions of cells that make up the human brain (see Figure 1). A quarter of a century of research on PS has established that it is the single best means for conserving memory and other higher brain functions through the passing of the years. What is more, PS is an exceptionally safe dietary supplement. An extra margin of safety comes from PS being more than a nutrient. Like the vitamins, PS is an orthomolecule.

This term "orthomolecule," brilliantly coined by the late Professor Linus Pauling, conveys that PS is "orthodox" to the body; that PS is found throughout the body as the same molecule that comes in with diet. This means PS is familiar to the body's defenses, highly unlikely to be seen as a threat and essentially free of adverse effects.

Actually, PS is universally present in living things from the most simple to the most complex. It is a phospholipid, one of a class of orthomolecules that went into the first cells. It is present in every single one of our cells.

Cells are the most basic functional units of life, and the human body is made up of about 100 trillion of them. They depend heavily on membranes for all their life functions. All cells can be simplistically thought of as "bags within bags." The bags define compartments within the cell that carry out specialized functions–divisions of labor within the cell. The bags are packaged by the cell's membrane system, and PS helps build these membranes.

PS has known functions in all of our tissues and organs but is most concentrated in the brain. There it facilitates the entire complex diversity of activities that make the brain the sophisticated organ that it is. PS works to functionally integrate the brain's different cells, tissue and regions into a unified whole. This holistic clinical effectiveness of PS grows out of its universal placement in all the cells of the brain. PS acts at the deeply profound level of the cell membranes, and its benefits from this subcellular level translate into impressive results at the level of the whole person.

As of mid-1997, at least 64 human studies had been published on PS, of which 17 were double-blind. The consistently positive findings from these studies establish beyond a doubt that:

• PS can improve quality of life in Alzheimer's patients.

• PS can turn back the clock on the nondiseased, aging brain, revitalizing its functions.

• PS can benefit depression, and help the individual cope with stress.

• PS helps normalize brain biochemistry and physiology at every level.

• PS is safe to take and has negligible adverse effects.

With almost 3,000 peer-reviewed research papers available on PS, science has some understanding of how it works. It is the single best nutrient (really, the single best means of any kind) for safely conserving and restoring crucial higher functions of the brain (what is considered "cognition"). The remarkable benefits of PS and its safety in use are now established beyond doubt. What remains is to spread the message to the people who can benefit from PS.

As unfortunately happened with so many other breakthrough nutrients, PS became available as a dietary supplement in the United States much later than in Europe. As early as the 1980s, a few brave U.S. practitioners were having success using PS on their patients. Advances in production technology have now made PS commercially available from a soy lecithin-PS concentrate, which is more pleasant than the archaic cow brain material (now outmoded because of the danger of "mad cow" disease). PS now has solid scientific status as the number-one brain booster.

PS GIVES THE BEST BOOST TO FADING MEMORY

A great deal of research has been done with PS since it was chemically isolated almost a half-century ago (in 1948 by Folch). The main areas of research on PS have centered around its involvement in the brain and the immune system, and on the "basic science" of how PS contributes to the survival and functioning of all known types of cells. The human clinical research with PS has now established its clear superiority as a nutrient that enhances brain function in people both young and old.

In the human studies that have been done, just about every mental function that could be measured was benefited by PS to some extent. Experiments with laboratory animals verified the human findings, and were strengthened by the added advantage of structural and anatomical access to the brain tissue. Results from powerful electron microscopy done on brain cells, from pulling apart cell membranes and putting them back together, and from a great variety of biochemistry studies done in the test tube have led to a rational explanation for why PS is so beneficial to human subjects.

PS also has been found to benefit young, healthy adults in coping with stress, and studies are in progress that may confirm that it helps children (more on that later). It's no wonder PS is being called the number-one brain booster–there's solid scientific data to prove it!

A REAL DIFFERENCE IN ALZHEIMER'S

Alzheimer's disease is a specific form of dementia. The term "dementia" is related to "de-mentation," loss of mental capacity. Alzheimer's features inexorable and progressive deterioration of the areas of the brain that control "cognition"–memory, reasoning and the other higher mental faculties. As the disease progresses the brain cells die, the nerve networks get progressively thinner, and symptoms worsen. The patient with advanced Alzheimer's may have only 20 percent of his original nerve circuitry left intact.

Memory loss is only one part of the Alzheimer's nightmare. Cognition is an umbrella term, used mostly by scientists to lump together mental processes that we normally take for granted, such as thinking, reasoning, learning, remembering, concentrating and translating our thoughts into words. Alzheimer's progressively takes away all these, and more.

Alzheimer's can come on gradually, then suddenly become evident: from being a little bit forgetful, the person can't remember where he lives. Older events remain intact in memory, at least for a while, but as symptoms get worse recent events are no longer recorded. Personality changes occur: a formerly easygoing personality becomes quick to anger. Only about 15 percent of the cases are possibly linked to "bad genes."

As Alzheimer's progresses, the afflicted individual has to be reminded about the most basic functions, like eating and washing. In the final stages, he loses weight and loses control of his basic functions. Later he becomes bedridden, and more likely to pick up an infection. The average Alzheimer's patient is dead in less than 10 years after being diagnosed, usually from pneumonia.

The double-blind clinical trial has become established as the "gold standard" for clinical assessment of any nutrient (or drug) that is claimed to benefit health. PS has been repeatedly subjected to this stringent level of clinical assessment in Alzheimer's, non-Alzheimer's dementia and memory loss linked to aging. Twelve out of the total of 17 double-blind trial conducted with PS measured its effects on memory and other cognitive capacities. Several were on Alzheimer's patients.

PS DOUBLE-BLIND TRIALS IN
ALZHEIMER'S DISEASE

1. Delwaide, Belgium. This was the very first double-blind trial done with PS. P. J. Delwaide and three co-researchers did this trial at the University of Liege in Belgium, and published their results in 1986. The patients were 35 hospitalized men and women, ages 65 to 91, all with mild to moderate memory and other cognitive loss characteristic of Alzheimer's. The patients were randomly assigned to two groups, then evaluated for baseline scores. Thereafter, the PS group was given 300 mg per day (with meals), and compared with the placebo group.

The patients were evaluated at baseline, then after one week and six weeks of dosing, and once more at three weeks past the end of dosing. Rating scales were used to make clinical evaluations. The Crichton Rating Scale scored orientation, communication, cooperation, agitation, mobility and mood, as well as bowel control, dressing, feeding and sleep patterns. Also used was the Peri Scale; developed by Delwaide and others, it is a 49-point, more sensitive scale than the Crichton. Also administered was the Circle Crossing Test, a test to pick circles out from other geometrical forms.

The PS group improved over placebo on all three of these measures, and on the Peri Scale the improvement reached statistical significance.* When the 49 items of the Peri scale were grouped into ten categories, PS was linked to improvement in all ten. The

---

*A statistical probability (p value) is derived which quantifies the probability that the observed differences could have occurred by chance. The lower the p value, the greater the chance that the observed difference is real.

From the statistical comparisons between any two sets of data, $p < 0.05$ (p less than or equal to 0.05) suggests a 95 percent probability or better that the observed difference did not arise by chance. A $p < 0.01$ extends this probability to 99 percent or bet-

authors commented, ". . . the changes observed in the present study reflect an improvement in behavior which can be useful for subjects and their families" (p. 139). After a period of only six weeks, PS had made a real difference to Alzheimer's patients!

2. **Amaducci, Italy.** In 1988, Amaducci's group, published another well-designed double blind trial of PS specifically in Alzheimer's. This trial was the Italian Multicenter Study of Dementia. It involved 22 researchers, working in seven Italian neurology research centers. The 115 patients studied were aged 40 to 80 (average age 62). They were given PS at 200 mg per day versus placebo, and the dosing period was three months.

Perhaps because the 200 mg dose of PS given in this trial was lower than usual, benefits from PS were not very clear by the end of dosing (at three months), but were more evident at six months (three months after dosing with PS ended). Benefits were particularly clear in those patients who began the trial with more severe cognitive impairment. Three months after these Alzheimer's patients ceased to receive PS, their scores on personal memory, overall memory and performance of everyday activities were significantly improved.

The experienced Italian dementia researchers who conducted this study concluded from their findings that PS does slow or prevent further cognitive deterioration in persons with established dementia. Particularly noteworthy from this study was that the benefits of PS could still "break through" clinically at three months after the patients ceased receiving it.

3. **Crook, USA.** In 1992, Dr. Thomas Crook and co-researchers from Vanderbilt University and Italy published their double-blind trial on Alzheimer's patients. Fifty-one patients were studied whose ages ranged from 55 to 85 (average age 71 years). This study was also conducted double-blind and randomized. The PS group received 300 mg PS daily for 12 weeks, while the other group took a placebo. Assessments occurred at baseline, then at 3, 6, 9 and 12 weeks.

---

ter. Most investigators accept the 95 percent level of significance, which amounts to a 1 in 20 (or lower) chance of being wrong. A p <0.1 level of significance (90 percent probability, 1 in 10 or lower chance of being wrong) is usually called a "trend." It can be taken to mean that a real difference exists between the groups, and that greater statistical significance could emerge if, for example, patient group sizes had been larger or measuring techniques more precise.

By week 12, the end of the dosing period, the PS-treated subjects showed the following improvements (statistically significant at p<0.05):

• Memory for names of familiar persons, e.g., clinic staff members.

• Recall of the locations of frequently misplaced objects.

• Recall of details of events from the previous day.

• Recall of details of events from within the past week.

Using sophisticated statistical sorting techniques, the researchers identified a subgroup who derived additional benefits from PS. These numbered 33 of the total 51 Alzheimer's patients, and were those who had relatively mild cognitive impairment to begin with. This mildly demented subgroup benefited not just on all the tests listed above, but on others, namely:

• Less inclined to complain that their memory was deteriorating.

• Better able to maintain concentration.

• Showed global cognitive improvement.

Benefits from PS were apparent as early as three weeks after the beginning of dosing. Also, on the computerized tests, the mildly impaired subgroup improved in: Matching First and Last Names, Recognizing Faces, Matching Names with Faces, and Word Comprehension Skills.

4. Cenacchi, Italy. The largest ever double-blind trial on PS was conducted by Dr. Teresa Cenacchi and her collaborators on Alzheimer's. This trial involved 425 subjects of ages 65 to 93 (average age 77+ years), recruited at 23 institutions in northern Italy and coordinated by a large number of investigators. All subjects had moderate to severe cognitive decline; very severely affected Alzheimer's patients were excluded. Also excluded were patients with Parkinson's, depression or so-called "secondary dementias."

The patients were given PS at 300 mg per day versus placebo for six months. They were assessed at baseline, then at three months after dosing began and again at six months. After statistical analysis, the memory and learning scores were significantly improved in favor of PS. The scores on withdrawal and apathy also indicated significant improvement for the PS group. The investigators concluded, "The resulting improvements in adaptability to the environment can have an important impact on the quality of life of such patients."

This Cenacchi trial confirmed the optimistic results obtained with PS in the previous trials. It made a unique contribution to the clinical experience with PS by establishing that patients taking commonly prescribed pharmaceutical drugs still tolerate PS well. The investigators searched thoroughly for PS-pharmaceutical interactions, and for any adverse effects from PS, and found none.

Judging from the outcomes of these well-designed, double-blinded trials on PS, conducted by excellent research groups, it is clear that PS can partially revitalize the cognitive functions that usually fail for Alzheimer's. PS can be expected to give the most benefit to those in the early stages of Alzheimer's. Yet high-technology "PET" imaging (positron emission tomography, which measures energy production across the brain) taken of the brains of patients with advanced Alzheimer's indicates that they too can experience substatially enhanced brain activity from PS.

STOPS MEMORY LOSS IN DEMENTIA

Many of the symptoms of Alzheimer's can be mimicked by other forms of dementia. All dementias involve memory loss, which can progress all the way until severely demented persons fail to recognize loved ones or even to answer to their own names. Along with memory loss, by definition the demented person also has major loss of at least one of (a) loss of recognition for familiar objects, (b) loss of vocabulary, (c) loss of motor functions, or (d) loss of judgment and adaptability. Alcoholic damage, circulatory damage as from stroke or long-term smoking, Parkinson's disease, trauma to the brain, certain legal and illegal drugs, HIV, even nutritional deficiencies, can cause dementia.

PS DOUBLE-BLIND TRIALS VERSUS DEMENTIA

1. Palmieri, Italy. In 1987, G. Palmieri and R. Palmieri and their co-researchers published the results of their double-blind trial. This trial was carried out simultaneously at three research centers in Italy. It involved 87 subjects with "moderate" cognitive deterioration of a degree corresponding to clinical dementia. The subjects' ages ranged from 55 to 80 (average 73.1 years). After randomization and baseline evaluations, PS was given at a 300 mg daily dose in comparison with placebo, and the evaluation repeated at 60 days. PS was then discontinued, and a follow-up evaluation was done 30 days after PS dosing was withdrawn.

In this trial, the PS group benefited on tests of attention, concentration and short-term memory. On the five-word memory test, the improvement of the PS group was very impressive. On the broader clinical assessment, PS improved activities related to daily living, and especially seemed to lessen the apathy and withdrawal to which people with cognitive problems are often found susceptible. Items that were statistically improved included self-sufficiency in activities of daily living; sleep disturbances; abnormal behavior; initiative; and the overall behavioral deficit, which was highly significantly improved.

The authors stated, "Phosphatidylserine appears to exert an action in two distinct contexts: one relating to the cognitive effects of vigilance, attention, and short-term memory, and the other relating to behavioral aspects such as apathy, withdrawal and daily living . . ." (p. 81).

2. Nerozzi, Italy. D. Nerozzi and collaborators published in 1987 the results of another double-blind trial conducted in Italy. This one involved 35 subjects, 60 to 80 years of age, recruited from retirement homes near Rome. The degree of cognitive loss again resembled clinical dementia, and approximated the patients in the Palmieri trial. Here also, the PS group received 300 mg daily versus the placebo group, and the trial ran for 60 days. The PS group experienced statistically meaningful benefit on delayed memory recollection.

3. Villardita, Italy. This was another multicenter trial. Published in 1987, it involved 170 subjects, ages 55 to 80 (average age 65.7), with mild to moderate cognitive deterioration. The PS group received 300 mg daily versus the placebo group, and the trial ran for 90 days.

By the end of this trial, 12 of the 24 tests reached statistical significance in favor of PS. Tests for Attention and Vigilance were all highly significant, as were the tests of word manipulations linked to memory. PS also significantly improved performance on both immediate and delayed memory tests. Villardita and collaborators concluded that PS benefits attention and alertness in subjects with more advanced memory decline. They suggested that if taken at earlier stages of declineprior to dementia, PS would likely save those cognitive processes that are often the first to go as dementia develops.

OTHER TRIALS WITH PS AGAINST DEMENTIA

Several other trials were conducted with PS against dementia, on a nondouble-blind basis. These trials and their results were as follows:

1. Moderate dementia: 400 mg PS per day improved cognitive, emotional and motor functions at 30 days (Rabboni et al., 1990, open trial). Worthy of note here, is that PS also lowered aluminum (a toxic mineral) in the plasma of these patients.

2. Mild dementia: PS improved short-term memory, mood and behavior (Caffara and Santamaria, 1987, open trial).

3. Mild to moderate dementia: PS improved memory and recall, also socialization and participation (Granata and DiMichele, 1987, open trial).

4. Mild to moderate dementia: PS improved cognition and behavior (Puca et al., 1987, exploratory open trial).

5. Moderate dementia: PS produced global improvement (Allegro et al., 1987, open trial).

Many people who are clinically healthy find as they get into their forties or their fifties, sometimes even as early as their thirties, that they are losing mental sharpness. They have ever more trouble to keep track of their glasses and their keys. They have increasing difficulty remembering names and matching names to faces. After reading important material, they forget it within minutes. They have difficulty making word choices–in animated conversation, they search their minds for the right word and can't find it. They know something is wrong. This is not necessarily Alzheimer's, but there are indications that those who perform the worst at this stage could be at increased risk for Alzheimer's.

Fortunately, PS has proved to be of consistent benefit to people with memory loss that ranged from mild to severe.

AGE-RELATED COGNITIVE DECLINE: BACKGROUND

Thomas Crook, Ph.D. is a distinguished researcher into memory and related cognitive processes, especially with respect to aging. Early in his career he worked at the U.S. government's National Institute of Mental Health (NIMH), where he pioneered new testing methods for memory and cognition. Dr. Crook was a major contributor of effective tests to measure Age-Associated Memory Impairment (AAMI), now called Age-Related Cognitive Decline (ARCD).

ARCD is a condition that is unique: It often begins at 50 or earlier, and can be detected in about half of everyone past the age of 60. Not classified as a disease, it is listed in the *DSM-IV* (*Diagnostic and Statistical Manual of Mental Disorders*, 4th edition), the Bible of neuropsychiatry, in the category "Other Conditions That May Be a Focus of Clinical Attention."

ARCD is formally defined as a condition closely linked to aging: one in which (a) the subject aged 50 or older complains of memory loss, reporting that his or her mental performance is noticeably less than it was when they were younger; (b) testing determines that cognitive performance is impaired; (c) no detectable disease that can account for this cognitive loss, nor any significant risk factors for dementia. The recognition of ARCD is not just an academic exercise–its definition grew out of Dr. Crook's extensive experience with sophisticated but commonsense testing of mental functions. This progressive loss of the brain's higher functions can bring considerable distress to many aging adults.

Over the adult life span, individuals who are otherwise healthy can lose roughly as much as half of their cognitive capacities. Fifty, give or take five years, is the age at which most of us notice that our mental functions are beginning to wear around the edges.

Crook and his colleagues have accurate estimates that more than 40 percent of people aged 50 to 59 show ARCD, as do more than 50 percent of people aged 60 to 69, and an even greater proportion of those past 80. They also have strong indications from their test data that those persons most measurably impaired by ARCD are likely to be at higher risk for developing Alzheimer's later in life. Without question, the individuals worst hit by ARCD have serious trouble on the job and in their personal life: they aren't able to function at anywhere near the level they used to, and their situation becomes a source of embarrassment. Yet the clinical experience with PS suggest ARCD is a clinically manageable condition, and perhaps can be reversed.

TESTING FOR AGE-RELATED COGNITIVE DECLINE

After Thomas Crook left the NIMH, he founded the Memory Assessment Clinics, Inc. (MAC). Headquartered in Bethesda, Maryland, MAC has a second facility in Phoenix, Arizona, and working affiliations with 12 academic research centers in the United States along with centers in 10 countries in Europe. The MAC are the finest memory testing facilities in the world.

Dr. Crook and his co-researchers in MAC led the way in refining the earlier generation of cognition tests to make them more relevant to real life. They painstakingly developed a battery of tests that are objective, are statistically precise, and yet are "user-friendly" to the subject being tested. The tests are completed by the subject sitting in front of a video screen, without need for computer sophistication.

As simple as the MAC tests are, they provide precise scores that help establish the boundaries between normal but age-related, and disease-related cognitive performance in middle and late adulthood. The MAC battery includes tests that measure:

- Name-Face Recall. Learning, immediate memory recall, and delayed memory recall (40 minutes later) of names presented together with faces on the video screen.

- Face Recognition. A good way to measure visual memory.

- Grocery List Selective Reminding. A list of 15 common grocery items is used to help assess verbal learning, and delayed memory recall (after 40 minutes).

- Telephone Dialing. Ability to memorize a telephone number, and keep it in memory while being delayed and distracted. In this test, performance of older subjects is more likely to be affected by distraction.

- Misplaced Objects. Placement and recall of keys, glasses, other common household objects within a computerized representation of a house. This test measures "verbal-visual associative" memory.

- Divided Attention. Measures reaction times related to simulated driving of a car, with radio weather and traffic reports as distractions while driving. Also measures recall of the announcements–"verbal-vocabulary" memory.

- First-Last Names. The subject is presented with a series of six pairs of first and last names, then given the last names and asked to pair them with the first names. This test also assesses verbal memory

One MAC test that has proven particularly valuable to assess memory power is Name-Face Recall. In this test, subjects are presented with live recordings of individuals introducing themselves by common first names ("I'm John from Boston;" or "I'm Jane from San Francisco"). Recall is assessed by reshowing the same individuals in a different order, stating the name of the city in which they reside, and asking the subject to provide their names. For Immediate Recall, there are three learning trials in which 14 name-face pairs are presented and recall is assessed. The total number of name-face pairs recalled is added up over the three trials. Delayed Recall is the score assessed after 40 minutes. Both the Immediate and the Delayed Name-Face Recall tests are sensitive measures of age-related memory decline.

The Name-Face Recall and other tests of higher mental functions from Crook's group represent a new generation of commonsense tests for higher mental functions. They give to Crook's findings an "everyday" relevance that can be used by real people to get a real idea of how their higher mental functions are holding up against the passage of time.

Decline in Name-Face Recall Is Linked to Age

On the first presentation subjects in their twenties can pick up about four name-face matchings out of 14. After the second presentation they have picked up about nine, then go up to 12 on the third presentation. The perfect score is 14, and we're unlikely to score perfectly in this test, no matter how young we are. But there is a decade by decade decline in Name-Face Recall: the scores of subjects in their thirties are less than in the twenties, and scores decline further in the forties, fifties and sixties. Subjects in their seventies can barely match one name with one face on the first presentation. Besides this age-related decline in Name-Face Recall, Crook and colleagues reported similar decade by decade decline on the Grocery List test.

The pattern of memory decline with age, as measured by Crook's group using Name-Face Recall, appears to apply across cultures. It has been documented in Belgian and Italian subjects, in San Marino and the United States, and in the Minangkabau people of Sumatra. Memory decline with advancing age also has been seen in other mammals. These observations were the necessary culture-independent "baselines" against which Dr. Crook and his colleagues could compare low-scoring subjects. Those subjects scoring significantly lower for their age group are said to have ARCD.

Though they are not demented, persons with more severe ARCD are likely to have major problems in coping with everyday life. They can develop fears that they have (or will get)

Alzheimer's; often they become depressed or withdraw from their social circle. They become afraid that deprived of their cognitive skills, they will be little more than vegetables. These people are the ones most likely to benefit from PS.

PS REVERSES MEMORY LOSS BY 12 YEARS IN U.S. TRIAL

By the early 1990s, the focus of clinical research on PS had shifted to the United States. Two double-blind trials were conducted by Dr. Crook and his associates at the MAC, and were published in respected U.S. peer-reviewed journals. Both were extremely well-designed trials, and their findings thoroughly confirmed the European findings on PS up to that point. Crook concluded that in comparison with the 100 drugs he had tested, the nutrient PS was the best thing he had ever seen for restoring memory loss.

The trial by Crook's team on ARCD subjects appears to be the best-designed trial of its type ever conducted. In addition to Dr. Crook's MAC, clinicians from the Vanderbilt University School of Medicine in Nashville, Tennessee, the Stanford University School of Medicine in Palo Alto, California, and researchers in Italy were involved in its design and completion.

The various research centers followed predetermined guidelines to recruit 149 subjects, ages 50 to 75. Great pains were taken to make sure that the subjects fit the necessary criteria, and that those with symptoms of depression, stroke and other brain damage were excluded. PS was given at 300 mg per day, in comparison with a placebo, for 12 weeks. Baseline assessments were done, then subjects were assessed again at 3, 6, 9 and 12 weeks, and at 4 weeks after the dosing was stopped.

PS was found to have benefit over placebo for the entire PS group, but the breakthrough finding from this trial was that PS greatly benefited a subgroup of 57 subjects. These were the subjects who were relatively more memory-impaired to begin with. They were slightly older at the trial's beginning, averaging 64.3 years versus 61.6 for the other subjects. They improved on:

• Recognizing faces

- Learning names and faces
- Remembering names and faces
- Remembering telephone numbers
- Remembering a paragraph recently read
- Locating misplaced objects (keys, glasses, etc.)
- Concentrating while reading, conversing, performing tasks

Besides their improvement on these specific tests, the subgroup with more severe ARCD experienced overall improvement in their cognitive functions, as assessed from detailed interviews conducted "blind" by trained interviewers. But the data on Name-Face Acquisition (learning to match names together with faces) proved particularly reliable, and the researchers decided to use this as a model to calculate just how much PS had helped the more affected subgroup.

The researchers were able to calculate that on this measure of mental function, PS had "rolled back the clock" by roughly 12 years. In other words, from being at a "cognitive age" equivalent to a person age 64, this initially more afflicted subgroup was restored, on average, to a cognitive age of 52. Dr. Crook and his co-authors wrote, "The magnitude of effect [benefit from PS] may be considered significant by many subjects and clinicians" (p. 648).

The success of Crook's trial built upon the results of a more modest trial conducted earlier on ARCD by Sinforiani and collaborators (1987). The practical nature of Crook's name-face matching and other tests of higher mental functions, supported by their sophisticated statistical analysis, gives strong support to their conclusion that PS can actually rejuvenate memory.

The double-blind and other clinical trials conducted successfully with PS on Alzheimer's, non-Alzheimer's dementia and Age-Related Cognitive Decline, when taken altogether establish beyond doubt that PS is a premier brain nutrient. These impressive clinical results are consistent with this orthomolecule being an indispensable building block for the hundreds of billions of cells that make up the nerve networks, which in turn are organized into the circuits of the brain's memory centers. Particularly if accompanied by exercise, lifestyle revision and a good diet, PS is the foremost dietary supplement to help individuals maintain mental fitness to meet the challenges of daily life.

HELPS THE BRAIN RESPOND TO STRESS

The capacity to respond adaptively to stress is essential to our survival, yet the brain is highly vulnerable to sustained stress of any kind.

The time-tested, biological pattern of response to a stressful event is called the "fight-or-flight" response. It is a process that helps living beings adjust rapidly to any challenge, and to cope superbly with any short-term emergency. But for humans living in today's chaotic world, fight or flight has a frighteningly negative side.

MODERN HUMAN STRESS RESPONSE: GOOD THING GONE BAD

Stress starves the brain. Stress reduces circulation to the brain, causing the fragile brain cells to be deprived of oxygen and nutrients. If the stress is sustained beyond minutes, these cells can be damaged and sometimes die. The cells of the brain are not only the most expensive to maintain, but the most vulnerable to stress.

As the hippocampus and the cortex sustain stress damage, memory and other cognitive functions fade. As other brain regions are affected, the individual can develop movement impairments and tremors or go into depression. No doubt about it: Stress from whatever source is potentially damaging to the brain.

Our nerve cells are among our most delicate and expensive to keep running. First, they are the largest cells in the body. Some motor neurons, since they start in the brain and go the periphery of the body, get to 3 or 4 feet long in the human and up to 60 feet in a whale. These cells are very busy and have to be constantly fed with oxygen and nutrients. Thus the brain makes huge demands on the body's resources: with only 3 percent of the body's mass, the brain consumes more than 20 percent of the body's energy.

As if all this were not enough for the body to handle, the nerve cells are loaded with unsaturated fats that make them extra vulnerable to free radicals and other toxins. This makes them uniquely vulnerable to toxic damage from agents such as lead and other heavy metals, aluminum, cigarette smoke, alcohol; and to abuse from poor eating habits, lack of exercise and poor circulation, blood sugar fluctuations, even over-consumption of prescription drugs. Even emotional stress is a toxic stressor to our nerve cells.

The memory handling cells of the cortex and the hippocampus are our "best and brightest" brain cells. They are a hundred times or more the size of a red blood cell and among the largest in the brain. They are some of the busiest in the body: each of these huge, branching cells carries hundreds, sometimes thousands, of chemoelectric impulses per unit time, continually pumping ions in and out and dealing with hundreds of chemical transmitter substances. No wonder, then, that it takes a lot of glucose and a lot of oxygen to run these babies; they're fine-tuned, big gas guzzlers.

Because these cells use so much energy, they are extra-sensitive to fluctuations in blood sugar, and to other influences that restrict circulation to the brain or allows toxins to reach the brain. Not surprisingly, therefore, they are the most vulnerable to sustained emotional stress.

WHY DO HUMANS GET ULCERS AND ZEBRAS DON'T?

The most definitive research on the vulnerability of the brain to stress has been done by Robert Sapolsky, Ph.D. Professor of Neuroscience at Stanford University, Dr. Sapolsky wrote a highly readable book called *Why Zebras Don't Get Ulcers*. I highly recommend this book to the reader.

Dr. Sapolsky's highly acclaimed research proves that the modern human existence differs from the zebra's or other wild animals in their natural habitat, because our modern habitat is so loaded with stress. While the zebra only has to deal with stress as a short-term, occasional event, we modern humans have to face stress continually. Unfortunately for us, our biological means for coping with stress have remained basically the same as the zebra's. In the face of chronic stress, our "fight-or-flight" mechanisms have become a liability and a trigger for illness and disease.

When the zebra senses the approach of a predator, his stress response goes into action: Adrenaline and noradrenaline surge into the bloodstream, alerting the animal to danger. Glucose comes surging out of the storage tissues into the blood to provide more energy. The heart beats faster and breathing rate increases to better transport oxygen and nutrients. Stress hormones divert blood flow away from his brain, and towards his muscles, to help him escape the imminent danger.

For the few minutes that it takes to deal with the oncoming lion, everything in the zebra's physiology is controlled by the stress response. The fleeing zebra's higher brain functions give way to naked instinctual behavior in order for him to escape this danger. Then things calm down for the zebra; he has outrun the lion, and he can go back to meditating as he grazes. For us, the situation is different.

IN HUMANS, SUSTAINED STRESS
KILLS BRAIN CELLS

The vast majority of us live in a state of stress, not just for short periods during portions of the day, but almost all the time. On almost every day of every month, the commute to work, the work environment and career challenges; credit card debt and financial pressures; relationship challenges, demands imposed by family and friends; all conspire to keep us wired. Adrenaline and other stress hormones are continually being released into the bloodstream, and the sources of stress are maintained for weeks at a time, if not for months and years. The fight-or-flight response, just one part of the life of the zebra, is the story of life for too many humans. We run the risk of becoming casualties of the stress response gone awry.

The modern human environment features stressful agents of all kinds. Even more, according to Dr. Sapolsky, if we even *anticipate* stressful events:

> . . . emotional turmoil, psychological characteristics, our place in society, and the sort of society in which we live–can affect very real bodily events: whether cholesterol gums up our blood vessels or is safely cleared from the circulation . . . whether neurons in our brain will survive five minutes without oxygen. . . . How many hippos worry about whether Social Security is going to last as long as they will, or even what they are going to say on a first date?
>
> *Why Zebras Don't Get Ulcers*, pp. 4-5

Dr. Sapolsky's first-class research makes it undeniably clear: We are in the process of being destroyed by the lives we live. The sustained emotional stress, our anticipation of it and our feelings of powerlessness, kill brain cells and especially disable the hippocampus. So also do the sustained chemical stresses: cigarette smoke, pollutants, toxins in our foods and a variety of food additives. Under sustained stress, the physiological fight-or-flight response becomes pathologic: It pushes the individual into disease. We become mental casualties of chronic stress.

PS HELPS REVITALIZE ANTISTRESS MECHANISMS

The fight-or-flight stress response is brought about mainly by the hypothalamus region of the brain, working in harmony with the pituitary gland and the adrenal glands. These are collectively called the HPAA, which stands for hypothalamic-pituitary-adrenal axis. Clinical research indicates PS may help revitalize fading HPAA function in the elderly, and so help in coping with stress.

One practical test of the adequacy of the stress response is the Early Cortisol Escape Phenomenon. In young, healthy people the oral administration of 1 mg of dexamethasone (DEX, a synthetic glucocorticoid) normally suppresses the production of cortisol and other adrenal steroid hormones linked to the stress response, for more than 24 hours. In contrast, many older people do not show this suppression by DEX. Called Early Cortisol Escape, this phenomenon is thought to indicate disintegration or dysfunction of the HPAA in the elderly.

Dr. Dina Nerozzi and co-researchers at the University of Rome published in 1989 that oral supplementation with PS (300 mg per day) for 60 days restored DEX suppression in a group of 14 elderly, institutionalized men and women aged 66 to 78. They suggested that PS was restoring pituitary function by stimulating nerve cells to organize into new networks, and/or by returning chemical transmitter levels towards a more youthful balance.

In another clinical study conducted along similar lines, Rabboni and his group in Milan reported in 1990 that PS normalized DEX suppression in all the patients who began their study with abnormal DEX resistance. They administered PS (at 400 mg per day) to 30 elderly outpatients diagnosed either with either (a) Alzheimer's dementia, (b) dementia resulting from stroke or (c) mild depression. After 30 days, PS had given benefit to all three groups. All nine patients with loss of DEX suppression at entry into the study had their DEX suppression restored after 60 days on PS.

These researchers were so impressed with PS that they commented, "... phosphatidylserine ... could open the way to a new therapeutic conception: the possibility of influencing the complex inter-relations between the neurological, immunological and endocrine systems."

In addition to revitalizing the aging hypothalamic-pituitary-adrenal axis, PS helps "tune up" the body's 24-hour daily, "circadian" rhythms. As we age, these rhythms tend to become less synchronous, resulting in sleep problems and sometimes also hormonal imbalances. Normally the anterior pituitary gland plays a major role in the secretion of TSH (thyrotropin, thyroid stimulating hormone), growth hormone (GH) and other hormones that coordinate these cycles. Masturzo and collaborators (1990) did an open, placebo-controlled trial on institutionalized elderly men with disruption of TSH hormone secretion.

TSH is produced in a daily rhythm by the anterior pituitary gland to stimulate the release of the important hormone thyroxin from the thyroid gland. Researchers in this field seem to agree that loss of thyroid sensitivity to TSH stimulation is linked to loss of sensitivity to DEX. Going into the trial, these elderly male patients (ages 65 to 85, average age 73.7) had no detectable circadian rhythm of TSH. Masturzo's group found that during the 30 days of the trial, the patients on placebo deteriorated further, while those given PS (400 mg per day) had their daily rhythm of TSH secretion restored to a level comparable with the young male adult controls (mean age 22.3 years).

In another study, published by Nizzo and others in 1978, PS administered directly into the veins of human subjects stimulated growth hormone release. This effect also was interpreted as a possible rejuvenation of the pituitary gland by PS.

PROMISE FOR ATHLETIC PERFORMANCE

One beautiful effect of PS as an orthomolecule is that it works to keep the brain's processes within normal limits, raising them when they are low and lowering them when they are high. So PS boosts the weak stress response in the elderly person, and calms down exaggerated stress response in the healthy young person.

The fight-or-flight response is a basic, universal response to stress of any kind, and occurs in response to physical as well as mental stress. Stressful conditions typically cause cortisol, ACTH (adreno-cortico-trophic-hormone) and other stress hormones to be released into the circulation, even in the young and healthy. Thus young men who vigorously ride stationary bicycles in the laboratory show a surge of ACTH and cortisol release as a result of their strenuous exercise. PS given to these athletes prior to starting to exercise produced an impressive degree of down-regulation of the stress hormones. PS may have the capacity to "normalize" the stress-induced activation of the hypothalamic-pituitary-adrenal axis.

In 1992, Monteleone's group in Italy reported on a double-blind, placebo-controlled trial of young, healthy men subjected to exercise-induced stress. They gave PS supplements (800 mg per day) for 10 days to these young men prior to their session of bicycling to near-exhaustion. PS was found to lower, by about 30 percent, the cortisol production normally associated with this form of strenuous exercise. These findings show that PS can soften the severity of the stress response in young, healthy people under stress. They are therefore consistent with the awesome capacity of PS to influence brain function at all its levels of complexity.

IMPROVES MOOD, FIGHTS DEPRESSION

A number of human studies conducted with PS prove that it will benefit mood and help lift depression. In a double-blind trial conducted on elderly women, PS brought about consistent improvement of memory and behavior (Maggioni and others, 1990). Ten women aged 70 to 81 (average 73.3 years) were studied, all hospitalized with major chronic depression. The minimum level of symptoms for these women was reporting depressed mood on the majority of days for two years or more. Typically, such depression is associated with changes in appetite and sleep patterns, fatigue, poor self-image, reduced concentration and feelings of hopelessness, to the degree that their productivity and social functioning are impaired.

Along with the depression of mood in these elderly women came depressed cognitive functions that mimicked dementia. The trial design was to first give them placebo for 15 days, then put them on 300 mg PS for 45 days. Neither the patients nor the psychiatrists evaluating them knew the placebo-drug sequence.

When scored on the 45th day after starting on PS, the patients showed dramatic improvement in their depression, as scored by the Hamilton Rating Scale. The statistical significance of the finding was very high ($p < 0.001$, less than 1 chance in 1,000 that the finding was due to chance). Their anxiety scores also were dramatically improved, again at p<0.001. PS also significantly benefited the memory loss linked to their depression, along with their attention and concentration. Their emotional functioning improved across the board, as did their anxiety and irritability. Their social interests and cooperation also were markedly improved.

Rabboni worked together with Maggioni to do their open trial with PS on three groups each of 10 elderly patients, (a) with Alzheimer's, (b) with non-Alzheimer's dementia and (c) with clinical depression. By 30 days into the trial, PS had significantly improved the group with depression. The improvements from PS were still in place at day 90, a full 30 days after the PS dosing (400 mg per day) was discontinued.

In an open trial (where both the patients and the researchers know what is being given and to whom) published some years earlier (1987), Manfredi's group obtained statistically significant improvement of various "psycho-organic" parameters in 40 women aged 50-82 (average age 72.7). These women were suffering from brain circulation problems arising from hardening of the arteries, with or without high blood pressure. The first group were given 50 mg of PS per day by intramuscular injection, as an addition to their existing drug regimens. The second group received the drugs alone. After 30 days, both groups had benefited: In the PS group 24 of the 25 cases had an "optimal" clinical outcome, compared with only 10 of the 15 given drugs without PS. In addition, the PS group had superior improvements in asthenia (weakness), insomnia, anxiety and capacity for recollection, versus the drug regimen alone (all p<0.05).

Findings from a 1995 trial by Gindin and collaborators suggested PS can improve mood in men. Already in 1981, Sengupta and fellow researchers had documented abnormally low PS levels in platelets and red cells drawn from subjects with clinical depression. This suggests that clinical depression could be functionally linked to PS deficiency.

Lowered levels of the chemical transmitter dopamine have been linked to clinical depression. In an exploratory open trial by Fünfgeld and Nedwidek, conducted in 1987 on subjects with dopamine deficiency, eight of the 12 subjects given PS showed improvement. Another patient improved when the PS intake was increased. This trial went for only three weeks; a longer dosing period might have produced benefit in more of the subjects.

In a previous study by Argentiero and Tavolato in 1980, subjects exhibiting motor impairment responded to intravenous PS (about 35 mg). As their motor performance improved, sampling of their CSF (cerebrospinal fluid, located in the spinal cord and ventricles of the brain) revealed elevations in homovanillic acid, which is a marker for dopamine. Supporting the findings in humans are the findings that PS elevates dopamine levels in aging experimental animals and revitalizes the membrane receptors for dopamine. In animals PS also activates tyrosine hydroxylase, a key enzyme for lifting depression.

HELP IN EPILEPSY

Phosphatidylserine can also be of benefit for abnormal brain seizure activity, as occurs in epileptics. Based on their previous findings that PS used in combination with GABA (gamma-amino-butyric acid, a nerve transmitter) could ameliorate experimental seizure activity in rats, Loeb and co-researchers (1987) administered PS and GABA to human subjects suffering from sporadic seizure abnormalities, for periods ranging from 30 to 90 days.

The combination of PS plus GABA worked against absence seizures; one-third of the subjects experienced a greater than 50 percent reduction of this seizure type. In a subsequent trial carried out by Cocito and collaborators (1994), a one-time oral administration of PS by itself did not work as well for seizures. This is not surprising, since PS is a fat-soluble nutrient and would be expected to require at least several days' dosing to build up in the nerve cell membranes. However, when given intravenously to rats the PS plus GABA had an immediate calming effect on seizure activity, as reported by Loeb in 1989. This effect could be achieved by combining GABA only with PS, not with PC or other phospholipid.

BOOSTS BRAIN FUNCTIONS ON ALL LEVELS

The benefits of PS are still not fully explored–no doubt more will be found. However, a large number of excellent experiments have been done with PS, and it seems PS works from the foundations of the brain all the way up to its highest pinnacles. As shown in Figure 2, the effects of PS at the level of the individual nerve cells are the basis for its effects at every level of the brain's organization, and ultimately for its benefits to the brain as a whole. Revitalization of the nerve cells, nerve transmitter effects, electrical integration across the brain and integration of the brain with the other organ systems, all are enhanced by PS.

PS IS A KEY BUILDING BLOCK FOR THE BRAIN

After a quarter century of research with PS on human subjects, laboratory animals, cells in culture and molecules in the test tube, it is clear that this nutrient plays a unique role in all living systems, and has profound value to the human brain. The key to understanding PS is to appreciate the wide range of benefits PS has for the individual living cells that make up this organ. PS makes membranes, membranes make cells, the 100 billion cells organize into networks, and these are the circuitry of the working brain.

Cell membranes are hotbeds of dynamic life activity, the action centers of all cells. Once provided with the nutrients they need, they keep their individual cells vibrant, and at the highest levels this vitalizes the entire brain. This is the scientific basis for the magic of PS: It is so important a building block for cell membranes, and membranes are so important to cells, that increasing

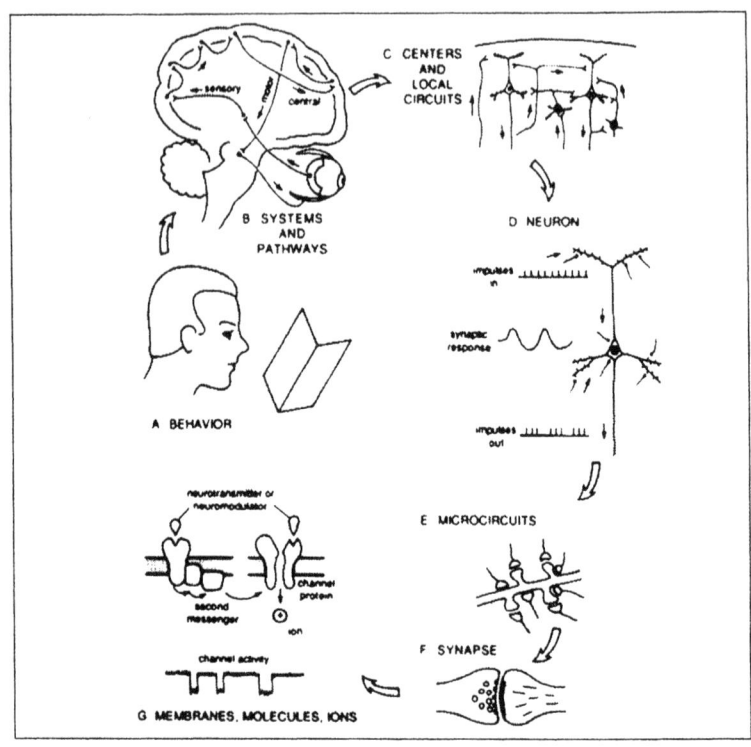

Figure 2. The levels of organization of the brain.
From Shepherd, 1988. *Neurobiology.*

PS in the brain can remarkably influence the performance of this entire organ.

PS is one of five major types of phospholipids (PL for short) that make up the foundation of the cell membranes. PS activates the enzymes and other proteins that do the vast majority of the cell's work, using the membranes as their work platforms. PS and the other PL are the main fabric of the membranes, the actual matrix that holds them together.

Each protein molecule located in the membrane matrix has specific chemical and physical associations with the phospholipids. These associations regulate its activity. PS is unique over the other phospholipids for its intimate involvement with many of the most important proteins of the membranes. Many PS molecules become intertwined with each large protein molecule, binding so tightly that they are pulled away only by the use of detergents. The nerve cells carry more PS in their membranes than do the other types of cells, and this may account for the exceptional effects of dietary PS on the brain.

THE SAFETY OF PS AND HOW TO BENEFIT FROM IT

PS is not abundant in common foods. Precisely because PS is found in all living things, its food sources are many, but paradoxically few foods except for brain provide substantial amounts of PS. According to rough estimates, all the PS coming into the body (mostly from muscle meats) hardly amounts to more than 70 to 80 milligrams, while clinically proven doses are in the range of 200 to 500 milligrams per day.

Moreover, the body can make PS only through a complex series of reactions and with substantial investment of energy. This pushes PS towards the category of "semi-essential" nutrient–a nutrient that the body may not make in sufficient amounts when aged, when under stress or when lacking in the necessary enzymes and metabolic cofactors.

PS IS EXTREMELY WELL-TOLERATED

PS has been proven safe in standard animal toxicology tests; dogs for example survived 70 grams per day of PS by mouth for one year. Out of the large number of human studies conducted with PS has come a flawless record of safety. PS is compatible with a wide array of drugs prescribed to the elderly, as reported by Cenacchi's group from their large double-blind trial. They allowed their patients to stay on such medications as antacids, anti-hypertensives, anti-inflammatories, antiulcer and mucolytic agents, diuretics, antithrombotics, hypoglycemics, antiarrthymics; insulin, calcium channel blockers, calcitonin and others. In 1987, a small open trial by Allegro and others had cleared PS of any adverse interactions with antihypertensive, cardiovascular, chemotherapy, diuretic or hypoglycemic drugs.

The Cenacchi trial also established that elderly patients (average age 77 plus) with chronic diseases tolerated PS well. Some of the disease categories they recorded in their patient population were cerebrovascular, artery and vein disorders, heart diseases, high blood pressure, diabetes, lung diseases, digestive system diseases and arthritis. Only one PS patient dropped out from a side effect (dizziness), versus eight dropouts from the placebo group. Cenacchi's group stated that "adverse events were very few, and clinically unimportant. These observations are remarkable in the light of the large number of subjects enrolled in this study, who represent a sample of the geriatric population commonly encountered in clinical practice" (p. 131).

As early as 1987, Cenacchi and her collaborators reviewed their laboratory findings after giving 300 mg of PS daily to 130 subjects for up to 60 days during clinical trials. They recorded lowering both of uric acid levels and of liver SGPT. Though statistically significant, these changes have no negative clinical significance; in fact, a lowering of liver SGPT could mean improved liver health.

HOW TO TAKE PS FOR BEST RESULTS

A reasonable supplementation strategy with PS is to begin at a higher level of intake (200 to 300 mg per day with meals) for a month or two, which should saturate the cell membranes, then to go into a maintenance mode at a lower level of intake (100 to 200 mg daily). There is no indication of potential problems from long-term supplementation with PS.

As a general rule, because PS is so safe, the more severe the person's problems, the more aggressive can be the supplementation strategy. Patients with Alzheimer's can be kept on all their other supplements and medications, and be given PS with their meals at 300 to 500 mg per day, on an ongoing basis. Patients afflicted with Parkinson's or other motor disorders may respond better at 500 mg per day. Anecdotal reports on stroke suggest 500 mg is a good daily dose until recovery begins, followed by a maintenance level of 200 to 300 mg per day. Anxiety and depression may require a starting dose of 400 mg per day. For age-related cognitive decline (ARCD), those with more severe signs should supplement at 300 mg daily for two months, then can choose to go down to 200 mg per day for maintenance.

People who prudently decide to take PS for a mental tune-up may find a 200 mg/100 mg schedule sufficient. From time to time, people with relatively severe clinical impairment will find intakes of PS higher than 500 mg per day to be useful, but (as with other nutrients) the administration of PS to seriously ill people should be conducted under the supervision of a qualified health-care professional.

During memory decline the earlier that PS can be started, or the sooner after brain trauma, the more completely it may ameliorate age-related loss of higher brain functions. A surgeon in Connecticut found that his patients recovered faster from "brain fog" following surgery, if he put them on PS as they come out of the operating room. However, it often is useful to start an individual on PS even at a late stage of cognitive loss, because studies prove that PS can benefit subjects with all degrees of cognitive, motor or mood decline.

PS was available commercially in Europe beginning about the mid-1980s, when savvy U.S. "alternative" practitioners were importing PS extracted from cow brain from Europe. Then it became clear that the European cattle herds were potentially contaminated by prions, the cause of "mad cow" disease. Luckily, new technology was developed that made it possible to produce commercial amounts of PS from a plant source. A soy lecithin-based PS concentrate is now available that is safe to take, and is effective for dietary supplementation.

Soy PS Is Just as Effective

In 1997 a brief debate occurred about whether soy PS was equivalent in effectiveness to the PS from cow brain. This debate was put to rest when Dr. Thomas Crook administered the Leci-PS™ soy PS concentrate to subjects with age-related cognitive decline, subjected them to the same memory and other cognition testing, and compared the results with those from cow brain PS. Dr. Crook found that soy PS gave just as much benefit as did cow brain PS.

The characteristic extra negative charge on the head piece of PS, combined with the unique three-dimensional shape, or "conformation," of the PS molecule are the keys to its specific actions (see page 6). These are the same, whether the PS comes from bovine brain or from the soy plant.

In various well-designed experiments, done both in the "test tube" setting and in laboratory animals, phospholipids other than PS failed to do the job of PS, as also did fatty acids, serine or other subcomponents of the large PS molecule.

A phosphorylated serine is available as a dietary supplement but does not substitute for PS, despite the claims of its manufacturer. Though it resembles the head piece of PS, phosphorylated serine is a different entity from PS and does not work like PS does. Consumers report it can cause highly uncomfortable adverse reactions.

Another debate occurred as to whether PS would work in the brain without having DHA in its tail pieces. DHA (docosahexaenoic acid) is a long-chain, omega-3 fatty acid. The two tails of the PS molecule are fatty acids. The tail in position 1 (attached to carbon 1 of the glycerol middle piece) almost always carries a saturated or monounsaturated fatty acid, and position 2 can carry a variety of fatty acids, including long-chain ones like DHA. Yet PS in the brain doesn't carry much DHA–at most, 10 percent of all the PS molecules in the brain have DHA.

The odds are very low that the fatty acid tails on a PS molecule are going to stay in position all the way from its oral administration through digestion and absorption, until the parent molecule reaches a nerve cell. Usually the tails are clipped off by digestive enzymes prior to absorption, then new tails are pasted onto the molecule following absorption. Thus PS in blood has different tails from PS in the testes or PS in the brain.

As recently absorbed PS approaches the brain, removal of tail 2 may facilitate passage across the blood-brain barrier. New tails are then added; the biochemical studies conducted by Dr. Lloyd Horrocks and others indicate that the nerve cell membranes continually are remolding the tails of the PS parent molecules to suit their functional needs.

A VALUABLE TOOL FOR ALZHEIMER'S PREVENTION

In any rationally organized program aimed at revitalizing declining mental capacities, supplementation with PS ought to be the central focus. The legacy of the extensive clinical research with PS is to establish that its use is essential in order to give the brain the best chance to wake up and be revitalized or in some cases even rejuvenated. PS is a logical first choice in efforts to protect persons with substantial cognitive loss against sliding down the steep slope into Alzheimer's.

The two U.S. clinical trials on PS conducted by Dr. Thomas Crook and his associates are probably the best ever done on memory decline and its treatment. These trials documented that PS could benefit subjects with ARCD as well as patients with Alzheimer's disease. The best results with the ARCD subjects were on those who had more severe age-related memory loss but who had not progressed to Alzheimer's. The best results with the Alzheimer's patients were on those with the mildest form of the disease. These clinical outcomes are consistent with what we know about how PS works; it would seem that the less severely the memory circuitry is damaged when PS is begun, the better the prospects for rebuilding them and revitalizing the memory.

After working with tens of thousands of subjects for almost a quarter century, Dr. Crook and his colleagues are probably the world's foremost experts at analyzing cognitive impairment. They are eminently qualified to comment on ARCD and Alzheimer's, having been involved in defining these conditions for the textbooks. They interpret their findings to suggest that subjects with

ARCD who score the lowest, as compared with peers in their age group, probably have a substantially higher risk of developing Alzheimer's. Once ARCD sets in, it would be prudent to begin with PS.

Alzheimer's is the ultimate robber. It features progressive loss of all the higher mental functions that make us who we are. As it advances, it takes away not just the mental skills but the very personality of the individual. By the time it kills the patient, it may have robbed him of as much as 80 percent of his brain circuitry.

Age-related cognitive decline or ARCD is by definition a "condition" and not a disease. Officially it begins at age 50, and its damage to the circuitry can approach 50 percent over a lifetime. According to Dr. Crook, the differences between Alzheimer's disease and ARCD are quantitative rather than qualitative. That is to say, the structural and functional changes seen in Alzheimer's and ARCD parallel each other, and Alzheimer's seems to be not particularly different from ARCD, only worse. This raises the specter of old Uncle Fred, who is only 52 years old but having lots of trouble remembering people he has met, being at real risk of becoming an Alzheimer's victim. The research suggests there is only a thin line between age-related memory loss and potentially debilitating dementia.

If by the tender age of 50, the earliest age at which ARCD can be diagnosed, Uncle Fred is found to be performing significantly more poorly on cognitive tests in comparison with his peers, he would be well advised to start on PS immediately. Along with taking PS, he can do still more to help himself through mental and physical exercise, dietary modification and stress reduction. He could take an all-inclusive, holistic approach to dealing with his problem, such as Dr. Khalsa's brain rebuilding program.

Dharma Singh Khalsa, M.D. is a well-rounded holistic physician, trained at the University of California San Francisco, Harvard and other elite medical institutions. He has founded a holistic program that uses a very wide range of activities to reverse mental decline. His vision is to prevent or delay Alzheimer's in the vast majority of susceptible individuals, and in this way to save tremendous pain and financial cost while swelling the ranks of the elderly with people who have revitalized mental function and wisdom to spare. Dr. Khalsa uses PS in his program, which has brought noticeable benefit to a number of persons previously considered pre-Alzheimer's.

A HOLISTIC STRATEGY FOR CONSERVING BRAIN POWER

The holistic way of living is the most healthy human existence. To live holistically means to integrate all the different parts of life into a harmonious whole. You get the odds on your side to become more healthy, to be more resistant to disease or infection, to age less rapidly. By living holistically you stand to gain more control over your life.

There's one hitch to adopting the holistic way of life: You need to use your head and really be involved. This is not something that someone can do for you. Your capacity to benefit from holistic living depends on your willingness to exercise clear thinking and good judgment. These qualities will help you deal with the factors that are within your control to change. Certain kinds of changes are almost guaranteed to help your brain power, as follows:

- **Keep the body free of damaging substances.** Scientific evidence indicates that memory decline is at least partly linked to harmful factors that are under the individual's control. The excessive consumption of alcohol, the smoking of cigarettes, preferences for bad foods, mercury fillings in the teeth, all are up to the individual to change. Smoking causes blood vessel damage in the brain, just as it does in the heart, and subjects the brain to massive free radical attack. Habitual alcohol consumption can cause a dementia as severe as Alzheimer's.

    Other toxic environmental factors are not totally under the individual's control to change, but often can be eliminated: lead and other toxins, polluted water, pesticides and herbicides on foods. Do not be distracted by talk about "bad" genes. As a rule unhealthy lifestyle and environment contributes far more to our risk of chronic disease than do our genes.

- **Use the brain—do mental exercise.** Ongoing mental stimulation is essential to rebuilding the brain circuits, because they give the brain positive input that the circuits are actually needed.

Here that old saying "use it or lose it" particularly applies: Use your brain cells, or you may lose them.

Play word games, card games, other games of concentration. Read good books. Memorize your telephone numbers. If you've suffered major memory loss, consider purchasing one of the reputable memory training programs and exercise with it every day.

- **Do physical exercise.** This increases blood flow to the brain, as it simultaneously helps the other organs. Lifting weights may not be enough; some kind of aerobic exercise is needed that really breaks a sweat, preferably three or four times a week.

- **Avoid sustained stress and low blood sugar.** Stressors, whether emotional or chemical in origin, lower blood sugar. This is extra dangerous to the brain, which uses more than 20 percent of the body's blood sugar while at rest, and even more while concentrating and doing mental tasks. Eat sensibly and regularly, to keep the brain smoothly supplied with the fuel it needs. Keep frying to a minimum: The brain is loaded with fatty substances that make up the nerve insulation, and these are particularly vulnerable to the free radicals that come in large quantities from fried foods. Use spices rich in antioxidants, such as garlic, onions, ginger, curry and rosemary.

- **Beware of excitotoxins in food.** These are nerve transmitters, and are essential to brain function in small amounts. But once their concentrations build up and they escape control, they can damage the brain. The nerve cells become overexcited, use up their available energy and eventually burn out.

One excitotoxin is glutamate. This can enter the body directly as MSG (monosodium glutamate), a food additive. Another is aspartate that comes from diet soda drinks.

- **Avoid drugs.** Legal or illegal, drugs pose a major toxic threat to the brain. Cocaine, amphetamines, psychedelics, all can kill brain tissue. So can marijuana. But one health scandal waiting to happen is that so many legal drugs can wipe out the memory. Some pharmaceuticals are as toxic to the brain as illegal drugs.

Many drugs widely used as sleep aids, antidepressants or

for other mood and behavior indications can have profound negative effects on the brain. According to the manual "Worst Pills, Best Pills II" from the Public Citizen Research Group in Washington, D.C., drugs such as Librium, Valium, Halcion, Prozac, Haldol, Xanax, Compazine, Stelazine, Thorazine and barbiturates are responsible for an estimated 10 percent of all the cases of dementia diagnosed each year. Many physicians fail to recognize symptoms of drug-related adverse effects, and instead diagnose their patient as having Alzheimer's or chronic depression. Patients lucky enough to be taken off the medication will sometimes partially recover.

Take dietary supplements, especially PS. Research findings that have accumulated over the past decade now make it clear even to the most skeptical among us, that dietary supplements are essential for good health. However well people eat, or think they eat, it is essential to add nutrient concentrates to the daily diet. Among many reasons for this are that poor agricultural practices have depleted soils of their nutrient content; the stresses of modern living increase our metabolic needs; and aging brings digestive and metabolic inefficiency.

Nutritional research at Harvard, Tufts/USDA, Berkeley, Stanford and elsewhere has moved beyond the RDAs, which barely correct deficiency states. Now the best researchers are working to determine the optimal daily intakes of nutrients - the amounts that help the individual feel really good, while also slowing aging and helping to protect against disease.

The brain needs all the nutrients that the rest of the body gets, because it too is flesh and blood. Some nutrients are quasi-vitamins, because they become lacking under circumstances of stress, aging, or toxic lifestyle. This is the category to which PS seems to belong, and at some point in our daily existence all of us probably will need PS.

Over the longer run, PS may prove to be valuable for many aspects of human health other than brain function. After all, this phospholipid is present in every type of cell in the body, and the membrane proteins that it activates are important in all cells. Already PS is known to be involved in bone matrix formation, testicular function, beat coordination in the heart, hormone secretion by the adrenal glands and the weeding out of dead and dying cells by the immune system.

CONCLUSION: PS IS THE NUMBER-ONE BRAIN BOOSTER

Alzheimer's is not inevitable with advancing age–many people in their nineties are still sharp mentally. But self-abusive lifestyle, environmental toxins, sustained emotional stress and lack of exercise all contribute to brain aging. These stressful factors work together to generate wear and tear on the brain. No doubt about it: as we age, we will need a brain booster to help us rebuild our brain circuits, or we could live long enough to lose our minds.

With almost 3,000 total research papers published, at least 64 of which were clinical studies on humans, phosphatidylserine is the proven number-one brain booster. The extensive findings on PS, published in peer-reviewed mainstream scientific journals, show that PS works consistently for the brain and that it is safe to take. That PS is an orthomolecule, meaning that it is intrinsic to all the body's cells, explains its impeccable safety record.

It is not a scientific exaggeration to conclude from the extensive research on PS, that it benefits virtually every brain function that can be tested. The key to PS being the number-one brain booster is the fundamental importance of cell membranes for life, and the importance of PS for cell membranes. The nerve cells' survival, housekeeping and high-level functions all involve membrane-based processes that rely on PS. This makes PS a far more complete brain booster than other nutrients–including B vitamins, minerals, antioxidants, herbs, amino acids, flavonoids and many nutrient metabolites–that do less for the membranes, or drugs which raise the levels of one nerve transmitter. While compatible with all these, PS is superior to them. By boosting membrane functions in cells throughout the brain, PS seems to boost many nerve transmitters while simultaneously boosting their coordinated effects across the entire brain. PS has clearly shown it can turn back the clock on brain decline.

Particularly when employed in conjunction with exercise and lifestyle revision, PS stands to improve quality of life for the young, the middle aged and the elderly. The wealth of scientific data on this remarkable nutrient indicates that however much damage to brain power an individual may have sustained; no matter how anxious or depressed they are; they will get some benefit from PS. Offering proven benefits that are not matched by any other nutrient or pharmaceutical, PS should be the foundation of everyone's personal program for conserving memory and other mental capacities so endangered by modern life.

One personal note to the reader: Whether or not you believe you are at extra risk for Alzheimer's, I guarantee you will benefit from a brain conservation program of your own. No matter how good you think your genes were when you were born, or how bad they may have become at this stage in your life, by starting on PS and taking other positive steps you can reasonably expect your brain power will get better. You can be sure that unless you seriously move to conserve the brain capacity you now have, you will have less to work with as the years go by. The earlier you begin on PS, the better.

REFERENCES

Allegro L, Favaretto V, Ziliotto G, 1987. "Oral phosphatidylserine in elderly subjects with cognitive deterioration: an open study." *Clinical Trials Journal* 24: 104-08.

Amaducci L, and others, 1988. "Phosphatidylserine in the dosing of Alzheimer's disease: results of a multicenter study." *Psychopharmacology Bulletin* 24: 130-34.

Argentiero V, Tavolato B, 1980. "Dopamine (DA) and serotonin metabolic levels in the cerebrospinal fluid (CSF) in Alzheimer's presenile dementia under basic conditions and after stimulation with cerebral cortex phospholipids (BC-PL)." *Journal of Neurology (Zeitschrift fur Neurologie)* 224: 53-58.

Caffara P, Santamaria V, 1987. "The effects of phosphatidylserine in subjects with mild cognitive decline. An open trial." *Clinical Trials Journal* 24: 109-14.

Cenacchi T, Baggio C, Palin E, 1987. "Human tolerability of oral phosphatidylserine assessed through laboratory examinations." *Clinical Trials Journal* 24: 125-30.

_____, and others, 1993. "Cognitive decline in the elderly: a double-blind, placebo-controlled multicenter study on efficacy of phosphatidylserine administration." *Aging: Clinical and Experimental Research* 5: 123-33.

Chen S, 1994. "Partial characterization of the molecular species of phosphatidylserine from human plasma." *Journal of Chromatography* (B) 661: 1-5.

Cocito L, and others, 1994. "GABA and phosphatidylserine in human photosensitivity: a pilot study." *Epilepsy Research* 17: 49-53.

Crook TH, and others, 1991. "Effects of phosphatidylserine in age-associated memory impairment." *Neurology* 41: 644-49.

_____, 1992. "Effects of phosphatidylserine in Alzheimer's disease." *Psychopharmacology Bulletin* 28: 61-66.

_____, 1993. "Recalling names after introduction: changes across the adult life span in two cultures." *Developmental Neuropsychology* 9: 103-13.

Delwaide PJ, and others, 1986. "Double-blind randomized controlled study of phosphatidylserine in demented subjects." *Acta Neurologica Scandinavia* 73: 136-140.

_____, 1989. "Effects of phosphatidylserine (BC-PS) on aged brain in normal subjects and senile demented patients." In *Phospholipids in the Nervous System: Biochemical and Molecular Pathology,* edited Bazan NG, Horrocks LA, Toffano G. Liviana Press, Padova, Italy.

Engel RR, et al., 1992. "Double-blind cross-over study of phosphatidylserine vs. placebo in subjects with early cognitive deterioration of the Alzheimer type." *European Neuropsychopharmacology* 2: 149-55.

Folch J, 1948. "The chemical structure of phosphastidylserine." *Journal of Biological Chemistry* 174: 439-50.

Fünfgeld EW, and others, 1989. "Double-blind study with phosphatidylserine (PS) in Parkinsonian patients with senile dementia of Alzheimer's type (SDAT)." *Progress in Clinical and Biological Research* 317: 1235-46.

_____, Nedwidek P, 1987. "Neurohomologous phosphatidylserine in Parkinsonian subjects with associated disorders of cerebral metabolism." *Clinical Trials Journal* 24: 42-61.

Gindin J, and others, 1995. "The effect of plant phosphatidylserine on age-associated memory impairment and mood in the functioning elderly." Geriatric Institute for Education and Research, and Department of Geriatrics, Kaplan Hospital, Rehovot, Israel.

Granata Q, DiMichele J, 1987. "Phosphatidylserine in elderly patients. An open trial." *Clinical Trials Journal* 24: 99-103.

Heiss WD, and others, 1993. "Activation PET as an instrument to determine therapeutic efficacy in Alzheimer's Disease." *Annals of the New York Academy of Sciences* 695: 327-31.

_____, 1994. "Long-term effects of phosphatidylserine, pyritinol, and cognitive training in Alzheimer's Disease." *Cognitive Deterioration* 5: 88-98.

Hershkowitz M, Diver A, Rabinowitz M, 1989. "Long-term treatment of dementia Alzheimer type with phosphatidylserine: effect on receptors and microviscosity of lymphocyte and thrombocyte membrane." In *Phospholipids in the Nervous System: Biochemical and Molecular Pathology,* edited Bazan NG, Horrocks LA, Toffano G. Liviana Press, Padova, Italy.

_____, and others, 1989. "Long-term treatment of dementia Alzheimer type with phosphatidylserine: I. Effect on cognitive functioning and performance in daily life. II. "Effect on receptors and microviscosity of lymphocyte and thrombocyte membrane." In *Phospholipids in the Nervous System: Biochemical and Molecular Pathology,* edited Bazan NG, Horrocks LA, Toffano G. Liviana Press, Padova, Italy.

Heywood R, Cozens DD, Richold M, 1987. "Toxicology of a phosphatidylserine preparation from bovine brain (BC-PS)." *Clinical Trials Journal* 24: 25-32.

Klinkhammer P, Szelies B, Heiss WD, 1990. "Effect of phosphatidylserine on cerebral glucose metabolism in Alzheimer's Disease." *Cognitive Deterioration* 1: 197-201.

Latorraca S, and others, 1993. "Effect of phosphatidylserine on free radical susceptibility in human diploid fibroblasts." *Journal of Neural Transmission* [P-D Sect] 6: 73-7.

Loeb C, and others, 1987. "Preliminary evaluation of the effect of GABA and phosphatidylserine in epileptic patients." *Epilepsy Research* 1: 209-12.

_____, 1989. "Antiepileptic activity of GABA and phosphatidylserine." In *Phospholipids in the Nervous System: Biochemical and Molecular Pathology,* edited Bazan NG, Horrocks LA, Toffano G. Liviana Press, Padova, Italy.

Lombardi GF, 1989. "Terapia farmacologica con fosfatidil serina in 40 pazienti ambulatoriali con sindrome demenziale senile." *Minerva Medica* 80: 599-602. [Translated from Italian]

Maggioni M, and others, 1990. "Effects of phosphatidylserine therapy in geriatric subjects with depressive disorders." *Acta Psychiatrica Scandinavia* 81: 265-70.

Manfredi M, and others, 1987. "Risultati clinici della fosfatidil-serina in 40 donne affete da turbe psico-organiche, in eta climaterica e senile." *La Clinica Terapeutica* 120: 33-6. [Translated from Italian]

Masturzo P, and others, 1990. "TSH circadian secretions in aged men and effect of phosphatidylserine dosing." *Chronobiologia* 17: 267-74.

Monteleone P, and others, 1990. "Effects of phosphatidylserine on the neuroendocrine response to physical stress in humans." *Neuroendocrinology* 52: 243-8.

_____, and others, 1992. "Blunting by chronic phosphatidylserine administration of the stress-induced activation of the hypothalamo-pituitary-adrenal axis in healthy men." *European Journal of Clinical Pharmacology* 41: 385-8.

Nerozzi D, et al., 1987. "Fosfatidilserina e disturbi della memoria nell'anziano." *La Clinica Terapeutica* 120: 399-404. [Translated from Italian]

Nizzo MC, and others, 1978. "Brain cortex phospholipids liposomes-effects on CSF HVA, 5-HIAA and on prolactin and somatotropin secretion in man." *Journal of Neural Transmission* 43: 93-102.

Palmieri G, and others, 1987. "Double-blind controlled trial of phosphatidylserine in subjects with senile mental deterioration." *Clinical Trials Journal* 24: 73-83.

Puca FM, and others, 1987. "Exploratory trial of phosphatidylserine efficacy in mildly demented subjects." *Clinical Trials Journal* 24: 94-98.

Rabboni M, and others, 1990. "Neuroendocrine and behavioral effects of phosphatidylserine in elderly patients with abiotrophic or vascular dementia or mild depression. A preliminary trial." *Clinical Trials Journal* 27: 230-40.

Ransmayr G, and others, 1987. "Double-blind placebo-controlled trial of phosphatidylserine in elderly subjects with arteriosclerotic encephalopathy." *Clinical Trials Journal* 24: 62-72.

Rosadini G, and others, 1991. "Phosphatidylserine: quantitative EEG effects in healthy volunteers." *Neuropsychobiology* 24: 42-48.

Sengupta N, Datta SC, Sengupta D, 1981. "Platelet and erythrocyte membrane lipid and phospholipid patterns in different types of mental patients." *Biochemical Medicine* 25: 267-75.

Sinforiani E, and others, 1987. "Cognitive decline in aging brain: therapeutic approach with phosphatidylserine." *Clinical Trials Journal* 24: 115-124.

Villardita C, and others, 1987. "Multicentre clinical trial of brain phosphatidylserine in elderly subjects with mental deterioration." *Clinical Trials Journal* 24: 84-93.

Zauli C, and others, 1984. "Evidence for a dopaminergic inhibitory effect of orally-administered phosphatidylserine on prolactin secretion in humans." *Neuroendocrinology Letters* 6: 37-47.

Milton Keynes UK
Ingram Content Group UK Ltd.
UKHW020621111023
430367UK00009B/236